ENGLISH SPRINGER SPANIEL

INTERPET
PUBLISHING

The Breed

The English Springer Spaniel has a long and fascinating history, but the breed was not officially defined until the nineteenth century. These early Springer Spaniels were used to flush out birds and small game and retrieve the carcasses. The Springer Spaniel was formally named in 1902 and recognized as a distinct breed. Springers are now one of the most popular breeds in Britain and America and these cheerful, affectionate and highly intelligent dogs make wonderful pets and hunting companions.

Published by Interpet Publishing,
Vincent Lane, Dorking,
Surrey, RH4 3YX, UK.

ISBN 978 1 84286 247 6

Printed and bound in China

The information and recommendations in this book are given without any guarantees on behalf of the author and publisher, who disclaim any liability with the use of this

Contents

1 THE HISTORY OF THE SPRINGER SPANIEL

Spaniels are the oldest breed of hunting dog, and were first described by Dr. John Caius in his 1576 Treatise of Englishe Dogs. Legend has it that spaniels were first introduced into Britain by the Romans, who brought the dogs from their Spanish colonies. "Spaniel" may be a corruption of either "espagnol", meaning Spanish or Spain, or "espanir," which is French for to "flatten out." It is thought that

ABOVE: *A well-trained Springer Spaniel is a joy to work with.*

the breed may have first originated in China, and made its way to Spain along the early trade routes. The Spaniel was definitely known in pre-Christian Britain, and is mentioned in Welsh law as early as 300 A.D.

It was not until the nineteenth century that Thomas Bewicke first defined both the English and Welsh Springer Spaniel, and the Cocker Spaniel breeds. At this time, English Springers, Welsh Springers, and Cocker Spaniels were usually born into the same litter. Litters were separated by colour (red and white coloured dogs were designated as Welsh Springer Spaniels, and dogs of other colours were designated English Springer Spaniels) and weight. Dogs over eleven kilograms were considered to be English and Welsh Springers, while dogs of less than eleven kilograms were classified as Cocker Spaniels. The heavier Springers were used to flush (or "spring") game, while the smaller dogs were used to hunt woodcock, and these animals came to be known as "cockers."

Springers were originally used to flush out birds and small game and retrieve the carcasses. Several hunting prints and paintings from the sixteenth

ABOVE: *The beautiful face and expressive eyes make these dogs welcome everywhere.*

and seventeenth centuries show dogs that are very similar to today's English Springer Spaniels at work, some of whom have docked tails. The invention of hunting guns in the 1600s greatly increased the popularity of the dogs, as they were so useful for flushing out game for the guns, and retrieving the shot birds.

In 1899, William Arkwright founded the Sporting Spaniel Society and this heralded a new era of pure bred dogs. In 1902, Springer Spaniels were formally named by The Sporting Spaniel Society of Britain. In the same year, Springer Spaniels were recognized as a distinct breed by the British Kennel Club. The first Springer champion was the famous Beechgrove Will, a liver and white spaniel dog owned by F. Winton Smith, who had been born in 1898. Fansome was the first Springer champion bitch. These dogs and several other notable animals founded the breeding stock that launched the modern Springer breed in Britain. These famous dogs included Champions Little Brand, Velox Powder, Rivington Sam, Rivington Bobstay, Springbok of Ware, Flint of Avendale, Inverisk Chanellor, Nuthill Dignity, and Rufton Recorder. These dogs are

7

still represented in the bloodstock of today's Springer Spaniels in Britain and the United States.

Spaniels have always been popular in the United States, and the American Spaniel Club was founded in 1881. Ernest Wells imported the first Springer Spaniels to the United States in 1907, and these animals were sold to Robert Dumont Foote of Morristown, New Jersey. The breed soon caught on and Springers were distributed around the country. The first Springer (Denne Lucy) was registered by the American Kennel club in 1910. In 1913 the first Springer was imported into Canada. At this time American hunters usually used pointers and setters as hunting dogs, but Springers soon became popular pheasant and sporting dogs. As a result of this, the English Spaniel Field Trial Association was founded in 1924. The founder members of the Association were Samuel G. Allen, William Hutchenson, Walter Ferguson, Henry Ferguson, and Alfred Ferguson. The American Kennel Club recognized the ESFTA in 1927 and adopted its breed standard for the Springer Spaniel. This breed standard was modelled on the Springer Spaniel breed standard of the British Kennel Club. This was revised in 1932 and revised again several times over the years. Over subsequent years the American Kennel Club has striven to foster the natural ability

LEFT: *Red and white coloured dogs were designated as Welsh Springer Spaniels.*

of the Springer, while encouraging uniformity within the breed. The Club maintains that American-bred English Springers should be black or liver with white, blue or liver roan, and tricolor. Lemon, red, and orange dogs are considered unacceptable.

Springers soon became one of America's most popular dog breeds with the same animals often being used as both working and show dogs. These "dual type" Springers were popular in the United States until the 1940s when show and working dogs began to diverge and breeders began to specialise in one or other of the types. In modern times hunting Springers are the ultimate in canine athleticism and performance, adept in flushing out both upland game and pursuing waterfowl. Show or conformation Springers, on the other hand, are fabulous examples of this highly attractive breed type and demonstrate its soundness and symmetry. The two kinds of Springer are now recognizably different in appearance.

For example, the coats of Working and Show dogs are quite dissimilar. Show dogs have a verdant, luxurious, and glossy coat with long feathers at the legs and around the trim. Working Springers have more practical and shorter coats. There is also a difference in the size and shape of the ears between the types. The ears of the Show strain are longer, with soft hair feathers. In the field, these beautiful

ABOVE: *Springers soon became popular sporting dogs in America.*

ears might get caught on branches and undergrowth. As a result Working Springers have smaller, flatter ears with few feathers. As Springers are great swimmers, the ear flaps also serve the important function of protecting the inner ear from water. It's best to keep the hair on the inside of a Springer's ear short in the summer. You should also check for burrs and seed pods caught up in the hair.

Both Working and Show Springers have deep chests and tail carried level with their backs, but Working dogs usually have finer bones and a lighter appearance.

Despite the differences between the two strains, all Springers are

ABOVE: *The working Springer has smaller ears than the show dog.*

beautifully proportioned dogs who carry themselves proudly.

Traditionally, Springer tails were shortened to prevent them from being damaged during their work in thick undergrowth. Such damage might affect the health and welfare of the dog. Surprisingly, Spaniels have actually been depicted with docked tails since the sixteenth century. In more recent years, Show Springers were usually docked to leave approximately one-third of the tail's length, while Working Springers usually kept approximately two-thirds of the tail length.

In Great Britain, almost all dog tail docking has been illegal since 2007. A few exemptions are made for working dogs, but the criteria are strict and tail docking outside of these exceptions is a criminal offence. The exceptions are defined by the Docking of Working Dogs Tails (England/Wales/Scotland) Regulations of 2007 and the Animal Welfare Act of 2006. It is forbidden to show a dog with a docked tail unless it was born before the ban was introduced. Exemptions to the docking law mean that both docked and undocked Springer puppies may be available for purchase. Docked puppies have tails that have been shortened within a few days of birth. These docked dogs are left with around a third of the natural tail.

Tail docking has also been banned in Scandinavia and most European countries.

ABOVE: *In the United States, tail docking is permissible and is usual for Springer Show dogs.*

11

ABOVE: *English Springers can be black and white as well as the more commonly seen liver colour.*

In the United States, tail docking is permissible and is usual for Springer Show dogs. Natural tails are considered inconsistent with the official breed standard. The American English Springer Spaniel breed standard states that Springers are "a medium-sized sporting dog with a compact body and a docked tail."

As far as showing Springers in America is concerned, a natural tail is a fault but is not a disqualification. Show judges evaluate a dog's positive attributes and then measure the impact of "faults," including a natural tail, on their assessment of the dog.

For many Springer enthusiasts, the joy of the dog is that the same animal can be both a working hunting or show dog and a great pet. Cheerful, affectionate and highly intelligent, Springers love their families and like to stick close to their owners. They are great with children and usually fit in well with other pets. Springers make excellent house pets, but require frequent brushing, combing and clipping of their silky coats to keep them neat and beautiful. They are also prone to shedding. Because of this, Springers benefit from professional grooming every few months. Having their coats professionally clipped or thinned out will make for easier maintenance. In addition, due to the very nature of these inquisitive little dogs and their love of water and mud, regular shampooing may also be necessary. You should also clip back the hair between the paw pads and on top of the feet as this can become very long. Keeping the hair on the paws short means that there will be less chance of thorns and burrs getting stuck in the hair and making the dog uncomfortable.

Springers' intelligence and sociable personalities mean that they need to be kept socialised and occupied to keep them happy and well-behaved. Dogs that are left alone for long periods of time, or unoccupied, may resort to mischievous and destructive behaviour or they may become nuisance barkers. Separation anxiety is a condition that affects many dogs from this breed, and it is definitely unkind to leave Springers alone for long periods of time.

Springers greatly appreciate being active during the day so that they can relax at home in the evening. Although modern Springer Spaniels are usually bred from either Show or Working dogs, their intelligence and trainability means that they can also make great therapy, sniffer, and hearing dogs. Their lovely faces and beautiful almond-shaped dark eyes are welcome wherever they go!

English Springer Spaniels have been consistently popular dogs. They rank around the twenty-ninth most popular breed in the United States, and are the third most popular dog in Britain.

One major reason for this popularity is the famous Springer temperament. Springers are almost always friendly and quick to learn, with a deep wish to please. They are adaptable and can live in apartments or country houses, so long as they are given enough outside exercise every day. Unsurprisingly, Working Springers need more exercise than their Show counterparts, so this might be a factor to consider when choosing your dog. But both Working and Show Springers are comparatively easy to train.

Health Issues

Although most Springers are very good natured, a minority can become aggressive and/or dominant as they mature. Of course, this can happen with most breeds, but Springer owners should be aware that they will certainly need to maintain their own dominant position as the "leader of the pack." However, there have been rare incidences of the so-called Rage Syndrome in Springers, which is sometimes known as "Springer Rage". In fact, the condition is almost completely exclusive to Show Springers and there have been no reported cases in purebred Working Springers. The problem is thought to be genetic in origin and is inheritable. It seems to be more prevalent in red, golden/blonde, and black solid-colored dogs, but this probably just reflects the fact that the condition is carried by certain bloodlines. Multi-colored dogs seem less susceptible. During an attack of Rage a dog will suddenly act aggressively to anyone nearby, but minutes later it will be calm and normal. The dog does not seem to remember what has happened and may be friendly to the person it attacked in the immediate aftermath of this. Unfortunately, these attacks cannot be prevented with training because the "Rage" is not under the dog's conscious

BELOW: *Most Springers are extremely good natured.*

ABOVE: *A classic liver and white Springer.*

control. Attacks happen without apparent cause, although an individual dog may have a specific trigger, such as being woken up unexpectedly. Prior to an attack the dog's eyes may glaze over and the dog may then become snappy before it attacks. Springer Rage can only be thoroughly diagnosed by a vet using an EEG or genetic testing and even these tests can be inconclusive. A variety of treatments including anti-epileptics have been reported to be effective, but not every treatment works for every dog.

Springers are also prone to a genetic condition that affects the skin, Ehlers-Danlos Syndrome. This is a disease of the connective tissue or collagen in the skin. The dog produces fragile, loose skin which is vulnerable to tearing and is unable to heal itself properly. The severity of the condition ranges from mild through to life threatening. Although there is no cure available for the moment, your vet can offer supportive treatment and corrective surgery.

Another negative Springer tendency is excitable or submissive urination (a tendency to dribble urine when excited or nervous). Although this isn't a major problem, you should take this into consideration if you are very house proud.

2 CHOOSING YOUR DOG

ABOVE: *A Springer can live to fifteen years of age.*

Springer puppies are so adorable that it is extremely tempting to scoop up one (or two!) and take them home. But getting any dog is a serious undertaking and you should be sure that you really want a dog (any dog) and that an English Springer Spaniel is the right dog for you. The issue of having time to exercise and give your dog the companionship he deserves is particularly critical to Springer ownership.

Most people buy Springers as family pets, but parents should be aware that they will almost inevitably end up looking after the dog, and will certainly be financially responsible. You should also remember that a Springer can live for fourteen or fifteen years, and you will need to commit to him for the whole of that time.

Once you have decided that you would like to take a Springer into your home, the next big decision is whether a Working dog or a Show dog would be right for you. The gene pools of

ABOVE: *Sometimes a puppy will seem to choose you!*

Field and Show dogs have now been separate for about seventy years, and both have different strengths to offer their new family.

WORKING/FIELD SPRINGER SPANIELS

If you are hoping to get a dog that will come shooting with you, a Working or Field Springer would certainly be preferable. Although Working Springer Spaniels are highly intelligent and easy to train, they have a lot of energy and may not make a relaxed family pet. However, if you lead a very active lifestyle and are outside for a good portion of the day, a Working Springer might be ideal. Like all Spaniels, the Springer is a people-orientated dog and doesn't tend to latch on to a single individual, but a gundog will naturally feel closer to his hunting companion.

SHOW SPRINGER SPANIELS

If you want to show your dog, or if you want an easy-going family pet, a Show Spaniel might be the best option. They are usually slightly larger than Working dogs, and will need more grooming with their thicker, longer coats. If you want to show your dog, you will definitely need to buy from a reputable Show line of dogs.

17

ABOVE AND BELOW: *A puppy needs to be walking before you can assess its character.*

RIGHT: *If you want an easy-going family pet, a show dog may be the best choice.*

DOG OR BITCH?

The personality differences between male and female Springers are quite subtle, and both make excellent pets and hunting partners. Many potential Springer owners are under the impression that Springer Spaniel dogs are likely to roam from home. This is not actually the case. Springers are not very prone to wanderlust, but bitches are more likely to have an independent streak. Of course, it is up to you as the owner to make sure that your dog is safely confined. Bitches may also be more stubborn and territorial and can be moody when they are in season. The other benefit of dogs is that you won't have to cope with their seasons every six months, unless you have your bitch spayed. Male Springers are usually slightly larger and heavier than bitches, and can be more exuberant. But they almost always have great characters and are very trainable, as well as being loving and faithful. Bitches can also be a little more demanding, and have their own agendas.

If you are buying a dog to be your hunting companion, a dog may be preferable as otherwise you will need to leave your in-season bitch at home for the duration of her bi-annual season.

Puppy or Older Dog?

One of the great things about adopting a grown-up Springer Spaniel is that you are probably giving a home to a dog that really needs one. There are many rescue organisations with dogs available in Britain, the United States and Canada. There will also be advantages to you. Your older dog may well be house trained (or nearly house trained!) and may also have been taught how to walk on the lead, and ride in the car. An older Springer may also be more appropriate for an elderly or infirm owner. You can also see exactly what you are getting in the way of temperament and size. The best way to find an older Springer may be through a breed rescue organisation. Dogs can end up in rescue kennels for many reasons, most of which are not any fault of the dog. For example, his owner may have died or become ill,

ABOVE: *An older dog may cope better if you are away from home during the day.*

ABOVE: *Dogs become homeless for many reasons.*

or a dog bought for showing may not have reached the required standard. Breeding bitches and stud dogs may also have been retired and would hugely benefit from having a loving and relaxed home of their own. One of the great things about Springers is that because they are such people-loving dogs, they will soon adapt to you and your lifestyle. An older dog might also find it easier if you are not at home all day and probably won't be as needy as a puppy.

Once you have decided what kind of Springer you would like to have, you need to find a highly regarded breeder. One of the best ways to do this is to contact an English Springer Spaniel breed clubs. Breed clubs often have lists of litters that have been bred by their members. If you can, it is highly desirable to meet the breeder before you decide to buy. A good breeder will want to know that you can offer a good home to one of their puppies and you can see the conditions in which your pup has been bred. Another good way of contacting breeders is to visit dog shows where Springers are being shown. This would also give a wonderful opportunity of meeting some Springer Spaniels close up and seeing the different sexes, sizes, and colours of the breed. The UK Kennel Club also has the Assured Breeder scheme where their members can offer litters on-line through their website. This is an excellent way of buying a dog for showing if that is your ambition.

But the very best way to find your puppy is by personal recommendation from someone who has already bought a puppy from a breeder. Naturally, if

ABOVE: *Visit your puppy a couple of times before he is ready to take home if you can.*

you are looking for a Springer to be a loving pet and companion, you need to look for a puppy from an affectionate and healthy environment.

Alternatively, if you want your Springer to be a show dog, you should try to source your puppy from a successful kennel. Breeders who sell budding show puppies will be well-placed to advise you about the potential of their puppies and give you an idea of how they will develop. A show puppy should appear balanced and attractive, and carry himself well. But buying a show puppy is always tricky. A puppy that looks like he has loads of potential at eight weeks of age may have faded by the time he attends his first dog show at six months.

A good breeder will also want to make sure that they are placing their puppies in good homes and should ask many questions about your home

ABOVE: *A reputable breeder will want to place their puppies in a good home.*

environment and lifestyle. If they do not feel that you can offer one of their puppies a good home, they may even refuse to sell you one.

If you are lucky enough to find a litter that has the kind of pup you are looking for, it can be a great bonding experience to meet your future puppy a couple of times before you take him home with you. It will also give you a chance to meet the parents of your puppy (or the dam at least) and this will give you an idea of how your dog will develop. You can also keep an eye on him to make sure that he stays in good health before you pick him up. This should be at around eight weeks old. A good breeder will be happy to welcome you to see your puppy and will be pleased by your interest.

What to Look For

Once you have found a litter from which to choose your puppy you need to use some objectivity to choose the right dog for you. In fact, there's

ABOVE: *You may be lucky and see both parents of the puppy.*

no point in looking at a litter prior to five weeks of age. You need to see the puppies on their feet before you can judge them properly. If possible, it would be great to see the puppies' mother and father. The main points to look for are your puppy's physical and behavioural health. So far as his physical health goes, there are several things that you should look out for. The puppy should have a good level of energy, and appear alert and interested in his surroundings. His eyes should be bright and clear without any crust or discharge, and he should be able to see a ball that rolls by slowly. He should look well fed, and have a little fat over his ribs. A healthy puppy's bottom should be free from faeces. His coat should be flat and glossy and not scurfy, dull or greasy. There should be no evidence of fleas or lice in his coat. He should be able to walk freely without any limping or discomfort. The puppy should be able to hear you if you clap behind his head.

A Springer puppy's head should show promise of a muzzle with a good length and he should have dark eyes (although these will certainly darken further with age). He should also have a level top line, a well-set tail, and well-developed hind quarters.

So far as his behaviour goes, you should look for a puppy that seems to be interacting well with his littermates - playing nicely without being too assertive. The puppy should also be

PUPPY LAYETTE

Before you collect your puppy, you will need to equip yourself with some simple pup-friendly equipment. His requirements will include a bed, basket, or dog crate a puppy collar and lead, a grooming brush, safe, durable puppy-friendly toys and puppy food (as per the breeder's instructions).

interested in playing with you and should approach you willingly. He should be happy about being handled, and let you cuddle him and touch him all over his body. If he remains calm and relaxed while you do this, he is likely to be easier to handle when he grows up.

Because Springer puppies are almost always so friendly, it may be worth looking at the slightly less effusive puppies who may be slightly less challenging and easier to train.

Puppy Diet

Most breeders will give you a diet sheet that should cover the first six months of your puppy's life. This will mean that you can keep the continuity of his diet which will mean one less change for him to cope with and prevent any unnecessary stress. Many breeders will give you some of the food they are feeding the puppy for the first couple of days. Give your puppy a small meal when you first bring him home, although he may be too nervous or tired to eat at first.

You may wish to adjust your new puppy's diet in time, but you should introduce new foods to his diet gradually. A puppy's stomach is quite delicate and can be upset by an abrupt change in his feeding regime. You will need at least two shallow-sided bowls for the puppy, one for food and one for water. Stainless steel bowls are ideal as they are both clean and unbreakable.

ABOVE: *Stainless steel bowls are ideal as they are both clean and unbreakable.*

Preparing for Your Puppy

You will need to make some important preparations before you collect your puppy and bring him home. You need to decide where you want your puppy to sleep, eat and exercise and which parts of your house you will allow the puppy to go. Consistent behaviour on your part will help your puppy feel secure and settle down quickly, so start as you mean to go on. All dogs need to have a routine and it is best to get this established as soon as possible.

Before you collect your puppy you must make sure that his new environment is free of any hidden hazards. Very importantly, your garden needs to be well fenced. A puppy needs only a tiny hole to squeeze through. Any openwork gates should have wire mesh attached, and any dangerous garden equipment should be put away. Indoors, you must make sure that electrical cables and phone wires are concealed.

Many house and garden plants are also highly toxic to dogs and puppies, and you should be very careful to keep them away from your Springer at any age.

DANGEROUS PLANTS

Of course puppies are much more likely to chew unsuitable things, so you need to be particularly careful that they are not exposed to a whole list of dangerous plant materials including:

Aconites	Box Wood		
African violets	Buttercups		
Apple seeds	Cherry stones	Daffodil bulbs	Ragwort
Apricot stones	Christmas roses	Elephant ears	Rhubarb
Crocuses	Clematis	Ivy	Wild cherry
Avocado	Cocoa husks	Mistletoe	Yew
Bluebells	(used in garden mulches)	Onions	

27

It is also a good idea to put away anything you really don't want to be chewed. You don't want to be telling off your new puppy on his first day in his new home.

One of the most important things to decide is where your puppy is going to sleep. This is crucial as this is somewhere that your puppy needs to feel completely safe and secure. It should be a place that suits both you and the dog. The most important thing is that the sleeping area should be warm, dry and completely draught free. Many owners prefer their new puppies to sleep in the kitchen or utility room as these rooms usually have washable floors. But you should not let him sleep in a confined space where there is a boiler in case of carbon monoxide leaks. You could also fence off a small area so that your puppy won't be able to get into trouble in the night. A playpen would be ideal for this. The floor of the pen could also be covered with newspaper. Although there are many different kinds of dog beds on the market, the simple plastic kidney-shaped baskets, which come in many different sizes and colours, are some of the most practical. They resist chewing and can be washed and disinfected. They can also be filled with cosy pads or mattresses on which the puppy can sleep comfortably. These mattress inserts can usually be washed in the washing machine. It's a good idea to buy two of these in case of accidents! An excellent idea is to replace the fabric softener in the washing cycle with a slug of disinfectant to make sure that any germs or bad smells are destroyed. Wicker baskets can be dangerous when chewed as the sharp sticks can damage the puppy's mouth or throat. Equally, bean bag beds can easily be chewed through and the polystyrene beans they contain are difficult to clean up.

ABOVE: *A puppy needs warm bedding that is easy to wash.*

Collecting Your Puppy

treatment and what vaccinations he has had. You should also receive a copy of your puppy's pedigree.

Although it is a very exciting time when you bring your Springer home for the first time, you should try to keep the atmosphere as calm and reassuring as possible. Moving to his new home is a complete change for your puppy and he has to fit into a completely new environment. Alternatively, if you are bringing an older dog into your home, he may already have insecurities that you will need to dispel.

The best age to collect your puppy is when he is around eight weeks old. When you arrange a time to pick him up from the breeder, a time around mid-morning is often the most convenient. This will give the puppy a good chance to feel at home by bedtime. He will be able to sniff around his new home, be cuddled by his new owners, eat, play and sleep before he faces the night alone.

It's a good idea to take someone with you when you go to collect your Springer puppy, so that one of you can drive and the other one can comfort the pup. An old towel to mop up any accidents is a good idea. When you collect him, make sure that you find out when he will need his next worming

LIFE CHANGES

Your puppy will have a lot of things to adjust to. At first, he may well feel lonely without his litter mates around him. A hot water bottle wrapped up in a blanket and a cuddly toy may help. Beware of going to your puppy if he cries during his first night with you. This is giving him the message that you will come running whenever he cries. You may also be tempted to take a miserable puppy into your own bed which you may not want to do in the long-term.

If you are re-homing an older dog, be sure to call him by the name he is used to. Trying to change it to something you prefer will confuse and upset him.

Caring For Your Springer Puppy

Now that you have brought your Springer puppy home, it's your responsibility to make sure that he grows up to be a healthy and happy dog. Good nutrition is one of the cornerstones of the care that he will need from you.

PUPPY NUTRITION

If you have bought your dog from a responsible breeder, they should have given you a diet sheet to follow. If you don't know what your puppy has been eating, you need to buy him some suitable puppy food. These foods are now sometimes breed specific. It is important that your puppy has access to water at all times but even more so if you are feeding dry food, as these foods can make your dog very thirsty. A common mistake is to give cows' milk to a puppy. This can badly upset your puppy's stomach and give him diarrhoea. Fully-weaned puppies don't need milk of any kind.

As your puppy only has a small tummy, you will need to divide his food into several small meals. Four meals are usually considered best for puppies up to the age of twelve weeks old; breakfast, lunch, tea, and supper. Serving small meals at 7a.m., 11a.m.,

3p.m., and 6 or 7p.m. works quite well. Don't allow him to go without food for more than six hours in the day. Leave his food down for around ten minutes so that he learns to eat up reasonably quickly. Don't worry if he doesn't finish his food at this age, he may just be full. Dried food will swell in the puppy's tummy and he will soon feel satisfied. Leaving his food down for him to graze on is not very salubrious. At this age, intervals of three to four hours between his meals should be about right. Once your puppy is three months old, he can move to three meals a day. By the time he is six months old, two daily meals will be sufficient. When your dog reaches his first birthday, you can move to a single daily meal if you like, but many people prefer to divide their dog's food into two meals a day. If you are unhappy feeding a complete dry diet, you can always supplement this with some tasty treats, but you should be careful not to offer your Springer puppy too much high-protein food as the breed can develop an allergy to these foods.

Most Springers have great appetites, and you shouldn't struggle to get your puppy eating heartily. Although complete diets are extremely

ABOVE: *Water should always be available.*

convenient, and contain everything your puppy needs, some owners prefer a more traditional puppy diet of various nutritious foods. You should not rely on a diet of household scraps as it is very unlikely that this will provide enough nutrition for your puppy to grow up strong and healthy.

ABOVE: *Find out what diet your puppy has been on from the breeder.*

HOUSE TRAINING

House training is the first sort of training that you should begin with your puppy. It should begin as soon as you first arrive home with him. With vigilance and positive training methods, most puppies quickly learn how to be clean in the house. Being a highly intelligent breed, Springers are particularly quick to learn.

House training will be easier if your puppy has a settled routine, sleeping and eating at the same times during the day. Puppies usually need to relieve themselves when they wake up, during play, and after meals. You should also watch for signs indicating that your puppy wants to go to the toilet; restlessness, whining, tail raising, sniffing and circling around. You should take your puppy to the same place in the garden on each of these occasions. You should encourage him with a consistent phrase such as "toilet." As soon as the puppy performs, you should praise him and play with him. You may be surprised how often your

ABOVE: *Take the puppy outside to his "toilet area".*

puppy needs to relieve himself, but remember he has only a small bladder at this age.

A puppy should never be chastised for making "mistakes". Instead, you should say a firm "no" to the puppy and take him outside to his toilet area. You then need to clean up as well as possible so that no smell lingers. This might give the puppy the idea that he can use that spot for his "business" in the future. While some puppies are easier to house train than others, you should remember that your puppy will not have full bladder control until he is about four months old and should never be punished for making mistakes.

ABOVE: *Puppy toys should be robust.*

PUPPY TOYS

Because Springers can be quite destructive, it is particularly important to make sure that anything you give your puppy has been tested to destruction. Pull toys can spoil his teeth, so these may be best avoided. Squeaky toys should have the squeaker removed in case this gets swallowed. Small balls are also dangerous. Large balls and chew toys made out of tough rubber are best and homemade toys such as cardboard boxes will give your puppy hours of harmless fun!

WORMING

All dogs have worms at some point in their lives, and puppies are at the most risk from infestation. Worms are passed from the mother even before birth and through their milk. They then live in the puppy's intestine and feed on partly digested food. Untreated worms can cause serious illnesses in puppies, including weight loss, vomiting, diarrhoea, a swollen tummy and even death. An infested puppy cannot get the benefit from his food and will not thrive. He may also cough and his coat may look dull. Puppies need regular worming to combat this and should be wormed from two weeks of age at two weekly intervals until they are twelve weeks of age, then every month until they are six months of age. Worming should continue at least three times a year with a recommended veterinary preparation for the rest of the dog's life.

Dogs are prone to two main types of worms, tapeworms and roundworms. Roundworms can appear like elastic bands, up to several inches in length. Tapeworms can appear like white grains of rice, which are joined together to form a tape. These are most commonly found in adult dogs and very rarely in puppies.

Your breeder should tell you about the worming programme they have been using and when the next treatment is due. Your vet can recommend a good product to use. Roundworms are spread through the environment while tapeworms are commonly spread by fleas, so it is wise to treat an infested dog with a flea treatment. Climate change has meant that dogs are now subject to new types of worm, Angiostrongylus, for example. These worms can live in the lungs or

ABOVE: *If you plan to put your dog into a boarding kennel, you will need to keep an up-to-date card showing the vaccinations he has had.*

in the major blood vessels and may even cause death. Ordinary worming medicine does not work against these parasites. You should check with your vet to see which worms are problematic locally.

One of the first things to do with your new Springer puppy is to get him used to being handled, particularly so that you can do essential things such as clean his teeth and cut his nails.

TEETH CLEANING

You can clean your dog's teeth with a special canine toothbrush, or a small piece of gauze wrapped around your finger. You can get special dog toothpaste from your vet (or on-line). This comes in various tasty flavours, such as chicken. Alternatively, you can use a paste of baking soda and water. Don't use fluoride toothpaste on puppies under the age of six months, as this can interfere with the formation of his dental enamel. Human toothpaste should also be avoided as this can upset your dog's stomach.

NAIL CLIPPING

Unless your Springer spends a lot of time walking on hard surfaces that will help to keep his claws short, his nails will need regular clipping. If you hear them clicking on a hard surface, it's time for a trim. Most dogs dislike having their feet handled, so you should try to get your puppy used to this from an early age. A dog's claw is made up of the nail itself, and the quick, which provides the blood supply to the nail. Avoid cutting into the quick as it will bleed profusely and is very sensitive. Don't worry if you can't do all your dog's nails in one session, it might be best to clip one paw at a time, with other activities in between.

INOCULATIONS

One of the most important things you need to do for your Springer puppy is to make sure that he is enrolled into a comprehensive vaccination programme. This will protect him against the serious illnesses of distemper, hepatitis, parvovirus, leptospirosis, and kennel cough. He will need regular boosters throughout his life. You should keep your puppy at home until he is fully protected.

Puppies should be vaccinated at 6-9 weeks of age and then again at 10-12 weeks. They will usually become fully protected two weeks after the second vaccination but your vet may recommend a third dose for some puppies. The vaccine your vet will use will contain a modified dose of the disease that will stimulate your dog's immune system to produce antibodies that will be able to fight the disease. If your puppy is unwell, it may be a good idea to postpone his injections for a while, to minimise the small risk of adverse reaction. Most vaccines are injected into the scruff, but the kennel cough vaccine is given as drops into the nose. The kennel cough vaccine is usually only given to dogs who will be left in boarding kennels, but it may also be useful if your dog needs to go into hospital for any reason.

When you take your unvaccinated puppy to the vet, you should make sure that you carry him and do not put him down in the surgery. If you plan to put your dog into a boarding kennel, you will need to keep an up-to-date card showing the vaccinations he has had.

Exercise

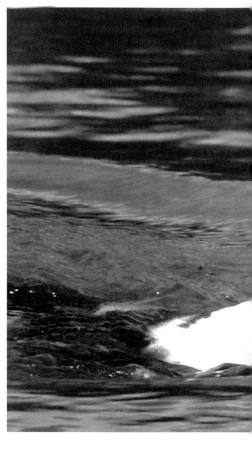

Your new Springer puppy needs to be kept both mentally and physically active to make sure he is stimulated and happy. But it is very important to exercise Springer puppies in moderation as his bones are still soft and growing. Over-exercising a puppy can lead to damage. This is an especially serious consideration in Springers who can be prone to hip problems and even hip dysplasia. This is a condition where the head of the femur is incorrectly shaped and will not fit into the socket of the pelvis. This condition can be aggravated by too much exercise at an early age. Most experts recommend that Springers should not be taken on long walks until they are around a year old and suggest around five minutes of exercise per day for every month of the puppy's age.

This would mean no more than thirty-five minutes of walking for a seven month old dog per day. By the time he is a year old, he can walk for hours.

As your Springer matures, exercise will become an increasingly important part of his day. Although he will

BELOW: *Springers love a swim, but you must remember to take a towel if you go in the car.*

appreciate long walks, he will also appreciate variety. You can also take toys with you on his walk, so that you can play with these as you go. Springers also love a swim, but you will need to take a towel if you go in the car. When your dog is a veteran, you will need to keep an eye on the amount of exercise he gets. Too much can stress his joints. He may benefit from taking more frequent, shorter walks. Swimming can also help, but a warm hydrotherapy pool will be more beneficial to his joints.

3 TRAINING YOUR SPRINGER

Basic obedience is important for any dog, but Springers particularly need to know who is the boss. As your puppy grows, it may be a good idea to enroll him in local obedience classes, but you can start his training the moment you bring him home to live with you. The essential thing to remember is that your Springer Spaniel puppy wants to please you, and so long as you remain patient, firm, and kind, he will learn quickly. Both Show and Working Springers need to learn the basics before they can go on to more advanced training for their special roles.

Springers are not only very intelligent, but they are also biddable and sweet natured. Although repetition is the key to training, your puppy will also need a lot of praise and reward to keep him interested.

The very first thing is to teach your puppy his name. You need to call him over to you with a treat in your hand, or be ready to play. You should sound excited and praise him lavishly when he comes to you. Do not ever call him over to tell him off, this will confuse him and make him reluctant to come to you on another occasion.

Before you move on to the next steps of training your puppy to sit, stay and walk to heel etc. there are some tips it is well worth remembering.

You should always make sure that you have your puppy's attention before you give a command. You should aim only to give commands that your puppy will obey, so you need to make sure that he is listening to you. You can do this by calling his name or snapping your

fingers until you have good eye contact with him. Then give your command, and make sure that your puppy follows through. Give him time to respond but ensure that he does as you have asked. Don't keep repeating the command as this means that your pup chooses when he obeys you. The idea is that he should obey you at once.

Puppies have only a short attention span, so you should keep your training sessions to no more than five or ten minutes. Your puppy won't be able to focus for much longer than this. It's important to keep the atmosphere of the training sessions as positive as possible, with lots of praise. If your puppy seems confused by a new command go back to something you know he can do so that you can end the session on a positive note. If you are using training treats as part of your method you may well find that it's better to time your sessions before meals, when the puppy might be a little hungry. But as your puppy gradually learns your commands you should phase out the treats, as you don't want to have to rely on treats in the long term.

LEAD TRAINING

Most Springer Spaniels very quickly learn how to walk on the lead. Their natural inclination is to keep close to you so attaching a lead to your pup's collar is usually no problem. Twelve to fourteen weeks is a good age for a puppy to start wearing his first collar. The puppy's neck will be very soft and delicate so you should use a very soft

ABOVE: *A secure garden is a good place to train your dog.*

and comfortable collar. Your puppy will soon grow out of this, so wait until he is at least six months of age before you buy him anything expensive.

The best place to begin training your puppy is in your garden. In this safe and controlled environment your puppy can learn about walking on the lead where there is nothing to upset or distract him. Encourage him and praise him as he walks well, but do not allow him to rush forwards and pull. If he does, keep calm and talk to him, then persuade him to walk a few steps and praise again. It will not take long for him to learn. Calm lead work will build a strong bond of trust between you so that when he goes out into the world and meets new and scary things he will look to you for reassurance.

TRAINING TO HEEL

The art of training your Springer to "heel" is a simple extension of training your puppy to work on the lead. The greater control the exercise gives you over your puppy is particularly important in an urban environment. A head collar or anti-pull harness can be helpful during heelwork training. The object of the exercise is to have the puppy walking by your side, with his head level with your left leg.

Start the exercise with your dog close to your left leg, with both of you facing the same way. Have one of your pup's favourite treats in your left hand. Hold the treat up near your waist, not directly in front of your dog's nose. Now say your dog's name to get his attention and to gain eye contact. Immediately take two steps forward and then stop. If your dog moves with you and is still in the heel position enthusiastically praise him and give a treat.

As soon as your puppy swallows his reward repeat the heeling process again. Say his name and take two steps forward while saying "come on" or "that's a good boy." Then stop, praise your dog and give him a treat. Only ever give the reward when your dog is still in the heel position. It's important to remember that you are using the treat to reward good behaviour rather than to lure or bribe him.

If at any time your dog lags behind or forges ahead of you hold off with your praise and rewards. Simply start the exercise again.

ABOVE: *Give the command "sit" and gently push the puppy's hindquarters down into the sitting position if necessary.*

TEACHING THE SIT

Teaching your puppy to sit is a useful exercise, as it shows him that you are in control. It can also calm a difficult situation. Most Springers will sit naturally just by voice. If, however, your puppy does not understand repeat the command "sit" and gently push the puppy's hindquarters down into the sitting position and then reward with a treat. The puppy will learn quickly.

TEACHING THE DOWN

The Down is the next command after Sit. Start with your puppy at the Sit position. Have a treat in your hand which you then hold on the floor in front of the puppy. When the puppy

goes down for it give the command "Down" followed by the reward and praise. When this exercise is repeated several times the puppy will go down without you having to put your hand to the floor, but reward and praise every time until it is firmly established. If the puppy will not go down at the start of this training you can give very gentle pressure on the forequarters to encourage him to go down to the floor.

TEACHING THE STAY

Learning to "Stay" is important to all dogs. When you first start to teach your puppy to stay it is best to have him on the lead. Ask the puppy to either sit, or go down, with the lead extended from you to the puppy; walk away backwards (facing the puppy) and repeat the command "Stay". When you get as far as the end of the lead, stand still for a few seconds, ask the puppy to come, and praise him. Gradually lengthen the distance you leave the puppy and always give praise when he does it right. If the puppy breaks the Stay take him back to where you left him at Sit or Down and repeat the exercise, but do not go so far away from him before you call him. This exercise will take time and patience; little and often is best. It may be helpful if you use a hand signal as well as the command.

TEACHING RECALL

Start to teach your puppy his name

ABOVE: *It may be helpful if you use a hand signal as well as the command.*

as soon as you get him and use it all the time, especially at meal times and when you give him a treat. Train him to come to you by calling his name and rewarding him when he comes to you with a cuddle or treat. This will soon become second nature to him. Coming when called is important for your dog's future safety and for your peace of mind so imprint it into his mind at an early age.

A good idea is to carry a treat in a crinkly paper bag. If your puppy doesn't come on command you can rustle the bag while you repeat the command. As soon as he has made the connection between the rustling paper and the treat he will always come to you. When he does you should stroke

and praise him.

If your Springer decides to disobey you use a low firm voice to get his attention. You don't need to shout! Once you have it you should immediately change your tone to a soft and encouraging tone and call him again. This should do the trick. When he has obeyed you give him a treat and praise him. You should also remember that however angry your dog has made you by refusing to come when he has been called, you must never punish him when he does finally come to you. This will confuse him and undermine his trust in your leadership.

A recall lead is useful for this exercise once you are ready to practise in an open space.

45

Springer Sports

The English Springer is considered to be the most versatile and trainable of gundogs. A Springer can learn to be a great gundog and remain a wonderful family pet. Springers can also learn to participate in obedience, agility and field trials. These disciplines are usually all-breed and your Springer could work towards various different awards: Companion Dog, Utility Dog, Working Dog and Tracking Dog.

AGILITY

The discipline of canine agility dates back to the Crufts dog shows of the late 1970s. To entertain the audience in the interval dogs ran around a specially designed course against the clock. The inspiration behind the concept was competitive horse jumping. The trend quickly spread to the United States and has now spread around the world. The sport consists of a dog and handler running around an obstacle course together. The obstacles are usually all different, but may include a variety of hurdles, an A-frame, a dog-walk, a see-saw, a tunnel, a long jump and a tyre. The competing dog/handler teams are scored for speed and accuracy.

The dogs participate off the lead and it is not permissible to encourage them with food or toys. The handler can only use voice and hand signals to instruct their dog.

ABOVE AND LEFT: *Canine agility was inspired by showjumping and quickly spread when Springers proved to be natural competitors.*

FLYBALL

Flyball is a modern variant of the sport agility that has become very popular in recent years. Essentially, Flyball is a sport in which teams of four dogs run in relays over a line of hurdles to a box where the dogs collect a tennis ball that they then return to their handlers. In Britain it is governed by the British Flyball Association and in America the sport is regulated by the North American Flyball Association.

As well as keeping dogs and owners fit agility competitions and Flyball can help to build the rapport between dog and owner.

Gundog Training

If you want to train your Springer as a gundog it would be wise to buy a dog from the correct stock. Your Working Springer's pedigree should include Field Trial Champions and Field Trial Winners. These titles may be abbreviated as FTCh or FTW. These dogs are usually smaller than their Show Dog counterparts. A puppy from a good background will very likely have a natural retrieving ability and a good nose to find game. Chances are that he will also have pace and stamina and be able to cope with both cover and water. Springers were bred to work with the falconer and the greyhound to "spring" game out of dense covers. Today's gun dogs are trained to find, flush and retrieve game. Springers were bred to work as gundogs and training your dog for this purpose is a great way of channelling his natural bounce and energy. In the UK the Gundog Club manages a graded training scheme for gundogs that was launched in 2006.

Many pet Springers have now joined this scheme on their way to becoming fully-trained gundogs. The scheme is suitable for pet dogs, working dogs and even show dogs. All true Springers have the instinct to retrieve and the training capitalises on their natural instincts. These intelligent dogs enjoy this kind of challenging training and working together will help you form a great bond of mutual respect with your dog. Many people have no intention of using their dog in the field when they start gundog training, although they may change their minds when they see how this work comes so naturally to their Springer.

In the first place, the best way to get your dog's training off to a good start is to join your local Gun Dog club. The good news is that you don't need to be a landowner to train a gundog. Most Gun Dog clubs will have access to a suitable piece of land, with differing terrain, where your dog can learn his new skills. This will include learning to Retrieve, Scent Discrimination and walking to heel off the lead.

The equipment you will need to get started is minimal – just a gundog slip-lead and a half kilo canvas training dummy. These can be found at country shows, gun shops or on-line.

Learning to Retrieve

ABOVE: *Toss a toy for your puppy to fetch.*

The lively and intelligent Springer has a variety of in-born skills and retrieving is one of them. But what if your puppy just doesn't seem interested in playing fetch? Even though nearly all Springers are born with an instinct to retrieve, it sometimes takes a little time and training to jumpstart this natural impulse. It might also be the case that, for a teething puppy who is still cutting his adult teeth, picking up objects with his mouth might be uncomfortable. Most Springers start to become more interested in retrieving at about six months old. Whether you are working with a puppy or an adult Springer the first step is to toss his toys and see if your pup shows an interest in running after them. It's more convenient to play this game in an enclosed area, like a hallway, where the dog can't avoid you after fetching the toy. When your dog

brings the toy back to you ask him to sit and gently take the toy from him. Then praise him and give him the toy back.

Once you have graduated from these first attempts to a training class, you and the other trainee handlers will be asked to make a line with your dogs. Dummies will then be thrown for you. Your job is to get your dog to wait until you are asked to retrieve the dummy. As soon as he does so you should make him sit still in front of you and gently take the dummy from him before giving him lots of praise. This training will continue until your dog can also retrieve hidden dummies, double dummies and dummies floating on water. As his tuition becomes more advanced your instructor may also encourage you to use a whistle, your voice and hand signals to communicate with your dog.

If you want to use your Springer as a gundog your pup will also need to become acclimatised to loud bangs and noises so that he won't be frightened by gunfire. A starter pistol that fires blanks can be a good way to introduce the noise of gunfire into the dog's environment. Try to "fire" at some distance from the dog, getting slowly closer.

As well as retrieving your gundog's

ABOVE: *Your dog can be trained to look for hidden dummies.*

training should include learning how to "quarter." This means working systematically in a zigzag pattern, covering the area ahead of you, while he is controlled by hand and whistled signals.

When your dog has matured a little, by about the age of around six months, you can attempt some more advanced training techniques including retrieving hidden dummies, retrieving from water and jump fences.

51

DUMMIES: TRADITIONAL VERSUS MODERN

The traditional gundog trainer's retrieving dummy is a half kilogram sawdust log. This is wrapped in plastic and then covered with canvas, often in a shade of aquamarine. An attached toggle makes for easier throwing. In America, most gundog trainers use moulded rubber or plastic dummies. These dummies are very light and easy to throw. Plastic dummies are often white. This means that they are easy to see against a background of earth, rock, and vegetation. As your dog becomes more advanced, you can use an orange dummy which is harder for the dog to see yet easy for you to spot. This will enable you to make more challenging retrieves without losing your equipment. Different shaped dummies are also on the market, while others leave a special scent.

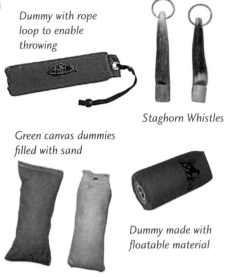

Dummy with rope loop to enable throwing

Staghorn Whistles

Green canvas dummies filled with sand

Dummy made with floatable material

ABOVE: *If your dog is to be used in the field he will have to become accustomed to gunshots.*

ABOVE: *Whether your dog hunts or not he will enjoy retrieving from water.*

The final stage of training your dog to work in the field is to begin shooting over your dog. This is probably the most crucial stage of gun dog training. Of course, this is potentially very dangerous, with even fatal consequences, so you really need to have expert tuition or experienced peer mentoring at this stage.

Many people have no intention of using their dogs for live shoots, but aim to train their dogs to a level where they can participate in field trials. Most field trial societies and clubs schedule special categories for puppies and novices as well as for more experienced dogs. Competing for the first time can be quite intimidating, but a good Field Trial society will try to make new members feel welcome.

When your dog has matured a little, by about the age of around six months, you can attempt some more advanced training techniques including retrieving hidden dummies, retrieving from water, and jump fences.

If you intend to use your dog in the field, or just enjoy a walk in the countryside, you must ensure that he knows not to chase game or livestock.

53

4 CARING FOR YOUR ADULT SPRINGER SPANIEL

GROOMING

Adult English Springers have well feathered ears and profuse silky hair on their chest, legs and tummy. This hair needs to be regularly groomed and kept clean and free from knots.

All Springers will require some degree of grooming to keep this coat in good condition. This needs to be done to ensure your dog's good health and maintain his appearance. Once you have decided what kind of coat you want your dog to have, you can integrate his grooming into your schedule.

There are three basic levels of grooming for Springer Spaniels. Working Springers are usually given a so-called "field trim." This is where the hair is cut short all over the dog's body and ears. It is designed to ensure that the coat does not become matted, dirty and uncomfortable when the dog is working outside in water and mud. Show dogs have a more subtle, sculpted trim in which the hair is left long on the outside of the ears and the leg feathers are left long.

Pet dogs usually just have their inner ear hair and the hair around their paws trimmed for their health and comfort.

ABOVE: *Springers need the hair around their toes trimmed.*

If you are going to take your dog to a grooming parlour, you need to specify that your dog should be cut with scissors and stripped by hand rather than with electric clippers. Once the clippers have been used, it is very difficult to restore his coat to its original texture.

Your puppy's coat will become much thicker from the age of about six months, and it is at this stage that you will need to get him used to being trimmed and groomed to keep an attractive appearance. If you plan to show your puppy, this is a useful opportunity to get him used to being handled, and it may be a good idea to get him to stand on a table while you work on his hair. So that you can give your pet a trim as easily as possible, you need to invest in a small amount of good quality grooming equipment. This should include:

- A pair of straight edged scissors.
- A pair of 30-tooth thinning scissors.
- A steel comb.
- A soft bristle brush or wire hound glove with a fabric back (for polishing the coat).
- A hard bristle brush.
- A slicker brush with metal teeth on one side.
- A stripping knife and blades.
- Nail clippers.

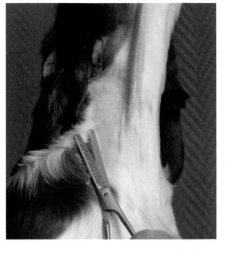

ABOVE: *Here thinning scissors are used on his throat.*

You may well find that a trimming table or a bench with a non-stick rubber mat would be a good investment. This means that you won't have to bend down to groom your Springer.

LEFT: *A trimming table with a non-stick mat makes it easier to groom the dog.*

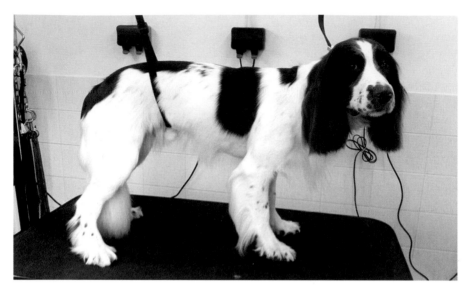

ABOVE: *Most dogs really enjoy the care and attention they receive while they are being groomed.*

Although you can soon learn how to give your dog a simple "pet trim," you may need more advice from your local breed club to give your dog a show cut. If you bought your dog from a show kennel, the breeder may also be able to give you a "show cut" tutorial. Either way, brushing and combing should be a daily routine. This will get rid of any dead hairs and any foreign objects lodged in the coat. You should always brush in the direction the coat is growing, and take care not to damage your dog's skin.

If you are giving your dog a pet trim, you only need to trim the hair inside his ears, on top of his head and ears, around his feet, and possibly the fur on his throat and chest.

The sooner you start to groom your Springer puppy, the sooner he will get used to this kind of handling. You can even pretend to trim him so that he gets used to hearing the scissors! Most dogs really enjoy the care and attention they receive while they are being groomed.

Start your grooming session by using the hound glove or a brush to remove all the dead hair and foreign objects from his coat. The comb will come in handy when you are tidying the feathers on his legs and ears. Be as gentle as you can during this process.

Inside of the ear around the entrance to the ear canal, the hair should be trimmed quite short to allow air to circulate freely into the ear. You should use the thinning scissors to do this. They can also be used to trim the hair on the outside of the earflap. The hair from the top of the ear to about a third of the way down should be thinned out. After thinning, use the comb to remove all the loose hair from the ear flap. At this stage, you can also carefully pluck out any dead hairs on top of the dog's head. Wearing rubber gloves makes it easier to get a good grip on the dead hair. Dead hair tends to look bleached out and will stick up on end, spoiling your Springer's sleek appearance. If the hair on the dog's chest and throat looks a little long, this might now be the time to thin out the hair in these areas. You can also trim the hair growing between your dog's toes and under the paws. You should use a pair of straight edged scissors for this.

A well-groomed dog does not need

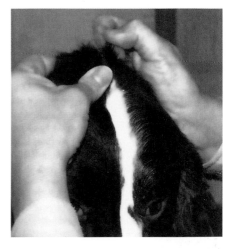

ABOVE: *The finger and thumb method can be used to pull out the longest hairs.*

regular bathing. This tends to strip the natural oils from his coat. But if your Springer has rolled in something horrid, you probably won't feel you have a choice. You should use a

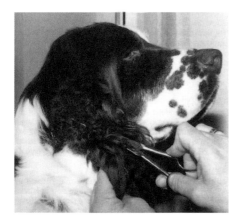

ABOVE: *Trim the hair on the outside of the ears, working against the natural lie of the hair.*

ABOVE: *Trim the inside of the ears so that they lie flat against the side of the head.*

ABOVE: *A well-groomed dog does not need regular bathing unless he rolls in something vile.*

canine shampoo and make sure that this doesn't wash into his eyes. Use lukewarm water to wash the dog, and make sure you rinse the soap out of his hair. Once you have towelled him dry (or dried him with a hairdryer) you should brush out his coat.

Unfortunately, a Springer's luxurious coat seems to be the ideal home for several parasites including fleas, lice, ticks, and harvest mites.

FLEAS
Fleas are small, flat, wingless, blood-sucking insects that are an irritation to dogs and their owners alike. They can also can carry and transmit serious diseases and other parasites (such as tapeworms). They are also the leading cause of skin problems in domestic dogs. Although they can't fly, fleas have powerful rear legs and can jump to extraordinary lengths. There are many types of flea, all of which reproduce rapidly and profusely. Despite its name, the ordinary cat flea is by far the most common flea that bothers pet dogs. Dogs become infested if good flea

prevention isn't followed. Dogs can also get fleas by having contact with other animals that have a flea problem. Fortunately, there are many things that dog owners can do to keep fleas under control. Most dogs that have fleas will find them irritating and will scratch, but some can have a severe reaction to flea bites (flea dermatitis). If you think that you have found flea debris in your dog's coat, collect some of the black grit from the coat and put it on a white tissue. If the black grit goes blood-coloured when you dampen it, your dog has fleas. Wash the dog as quickly as possible, not forgetting his bedding and around the house. There are many excellent flea-control preparations on the market today, but your vet will probably be able to sell you the most effective.

TICKS

Ticks can sometimes be found in your dog's coat in the summer months. Ticks are parasites of sheep and cattle. The adult tick starts life small and spider-like. It crawls over the body, finds a suitable place and bites into the skin. It will stay in this position for about two weeks until fully engorged with blood, swollen to the size of a pea and beige in colour. The tick will then drop off the host and, if female, lay eggs in the grass. These hatch into larvae which will then find a host. After a feed, these larvae drop off, undergo change and find another host. It takes three larvae

changes, each taking a year, before the adult form is arrived at and the cycle is then repeated. Ticks can be removed by using flea-control remedies, some of which are also designed to remove ticks. Other methods involve removing the tick with special forceps, making sure you grasp the head. This is made easier by killing the tick first. If you don't manage to remove the tick's mouth parts, the bite can become infected.

LICE

Lice are grey, about 2mm long and they lay small eggs (nits) which stick to the dog's hair and can look like scurf. Dogs can then scratch and create bald patches. You should give your dog repeat treatments of insecticide sprays or baths to kill the adults and any hatching larvae.

HARVEST MITES

Harvest mites infestation occurs in the late summer, starting around late July. They are little orange mites which affect the feet, legs and skin of the tummy and can cause immense irritation. The orange mite can just be seen with a naked eye. Treat with benzyl benzoate, a white emulsion which can be bought at the chemist, which should be rubbed into the affected parts. Many of the flea insecticides will also treat this complaint.

EARS

You can also use your grooming time to keep an eye on your Springer's ears. If your dog is scratching, shaking his head and holding an ear slightly away from the head, this might mean that your dog has got ear trouble and if this is the case you need to consult your vet. You can also buy special ear cleaners that help to clear excessive ear wax.

NAILS

If you walk your dog on hard surfaces, you may be able to keep his nails short just by doing this. But if you mostly walk your dog in the country, you should budget to clip his nails regularly. If you do this every one or two weeks, you will only need to remove the nail tips to keep them comfortable for him.

This will also prevent him developing a splay-footed appearance and suffering discomfort from excessively long nails. You must take every precaution to avoid cutting into the quick of the nail, as this will be very painful for your dog. In Britain, some Springers will have had their dewclaws removed, but many dogs will still have them. In America, these are more usually removed.

FEET

A Springer's feet need some attention to keep your dog happy and comfortable. It is particularly important to keep the hair on your dog's feet free of seeds and burrs as these can enter the paw itself and make him go lame.

TEETH AND GUMS

A Springer will usually get his adult

ABOVE AND RIGHT: *Consult your vet if you spot any problems with your dog's teeth or eyes.*

Tooth and gum massage should be done twice a week. You can use a bristle toothbrush and canine toothpaste.

EYES
Your Springer's eyes should always be bright and clear and free from any foreign objects. You need to check your dog's eyes regularly as eye problems can be indicative of other health problems. You should watch out for excessive crustiness, tearing, red or white eyelid linings, tear-stained hair, closed eyes, cloudiness, a visible third eyelid, or unequal pupil size. If you see any of these eye symptoms, you should contact your vet immediately.

teeth at around the age of four-and-a-half months. You need to check which puppy teeth are loose and which have fallen out, and to see how the new ones are coming on. Gently lift the lips to check the teeth. Be especially careful if your puppy is teething. It is good to get your puppy used to this procedure so that both you and your vet will be able to examine his mouth without too much trouble. You should check the tongue to make sure that it looks normal, and check the dog's teeth and gums. The teeth should be clean and free from tartar. If tartar builds up on the teeth his breath will smell, the teeth will become discoloured and eventually the gums will be affected, leading to infection.

The Veteran Springer

To many people the veteran Springer Spaniel becomes more precious as he ages. He will have given the best years of his life to be your companion. There are still some lovely times that you can have together. Springers can live to a good age. Twelve to fourteen years is typical and they have been known to achieve even greater ages.

As your dog ages his needs will change and the way you care for him will need to keep up with this. Good sense will tell you how much exercise he wants. A dog over the age of ten should be taken for shorter walks at his old pace. Of course, each dog will age at his own rate, so discretion and discernment is required.

Diet is perhaps one of the important changes you will notice as your dog ages. He will no longer require as much food. Teeth may not be as good as they were, so an entirely hard diet may no longer be suitable. It might also suit your older dog to eat two smaller meals each day so that his digestive system can cope better. Many dog food manufacturers offer diets that have been specially designed for the older dog. These may well be appropriate for your older Springer.

If your dog is taking less exercise you may also find that you need to trim his nails more often, and you need to make absolutely sure that you keep his coat clean and comfortable. Grooming will also give you a chance to check him over and notice any health problems at an early stage.

Older Springers should always be kept comfortable and warm. You should never allow your older dog to get cold and wet. Make sure his bed is somewhere where the temperature is constant and free of draughts. He will sleep longer and more soundly than when he was younger. If you have younger dogs in the family make sure the old dog is not left out but, at the same time, do not let the young dogs either annoy or disturb the old dog when he is sleeping. You should also protect the old dog from any boisterous activities from the younger dogs.

Finally, if your Springer is failing in health and losing his quality of life you may need to consider putting him to sleep. Your vet will help you make that decision when the time comes. It is the hardest decision to make but don't let your dog suffer at the end; you owe it to him to have a dignified departure from the world.

5 SHOWING YOUR SPRINGER SPANIEL

If you have bought your Springer puppy from a line of Show dogs, you may wish to show him. This will mean that your dog will be compared to the Springer Spaniel breed standard. This lays down the ideal character, temperament and appearance by which your dog will be judged.

The first thing that any good judge will be looking for is a sound and

healthy dog that is a good example of the breed. No reputable breeder would allow an unhealthy dog, or a dog with health issues to produce a litter.

In temperament, a good Springer should be demonstrably extrovert, friendly, happy and biddable. Any sign of timidity or aggression is totally out of character for this breed. His general appearance should also be merry and active, with a friendly wagging tail. Your dog should look strong, sturdy, compact, and well-balanced and he should have a proud and upstanding carriage. His overall "look" should be muscular, suggesting both stamina and agility. In both Britain and America the Ideal height for a Springer is 51 cm (20 ins) at the shoulder for a dog and 48cm (19ins) for a bitch. A dog should weigh around 25kg (55lbs), and a bitch should weigh around 20kg (44lbs).

Your Springer's gait should be sound and well balanced. He should have a long stride and driving power at the back. High-stepping and a choppy stride are considered faults.

THE HEAD

A Springer's head should be impressive but not too heavy. Its overall appearance should be strong but refined, with fine moulding around the eye sockets.

THE EYES

The Springer's eyes are the essence of the dog's appeal, with their trusting and clever expression. They are medium-sized, almond shaped, and dark hazel in colour.

THE EARS

The Springer's ears should be level with their eyes, and should hang loosely, reaching the tip of the dog's nose.

ABOVE: *Your dog should demonstrate stamina and agility.*

ABOVE: *The coat should be windproof and thorn proof.*

THE MOUTH

The Springer's mouth needs to be long enough to carry game easily and the jaw should be strong. The lower jaw should be covered by the upper lip. The teeth should be strong and clean. The upper teeth should overlap the lower ones in a close scissor bite.

THE BODY

The body should be short-coupled, strong and compact with a deep and well developed chest. The neck should be strong and muscular and moderately long. The front legs should be set under the body and they should be straight, with flat shoulder blades. The hindquarters should be muscular with strength and driving power. The feet should be compact and well-rounded, they are usually smaller at the back than at the front. The thighs should be broad and well developed.

THE TAIL

A Springer should have a merry tail that should be carried horizontally. It should be well feathered.

TESTICLES

Male Springer should have two testicles fully descended into the scrotum.

THE COAT

Springers have both outer and undercoats. The outer coat should be of a medium length and flat or wavy. The under coat is short, soft and dense. A good Springer should be feathered on the ears, chest, legs and stomach. The coat should be windproof and thorn proof. The overall appearance should be glossy and the coat should be trimmed lightly to give the dog a natural appearance. In Britain, the approved Springer colours are black or liver and white, and black or liver and white with tan markings. In America, blue or liver roan dogs are also acceptable. Lemon, red and orange dogs do not conform to show standards. A Springer's coat should be thinned and trimmed about a week before a show and (If necessary) bathed the day before. You should concentrate on the head, ears, throat, chin, hocks, backside and feet.

ABOVE: *A Springer's coat should be thinned and trimmed about a week before a show.*

Showing your dog can be a great way to make new friends and can be a highly absorbing hobby. There are all kinds of dog shows from the informal to the highly competitive and there are also parallel events for young dog handlers. So long as you approach dog shows with good sportsmanship and a sense of humour they can be great fun. You will need a small amount of equipment to show your dog. This should include a good grooming kit, a show lead, and a water bowl. You may find it safe and convenient to take your dog to shows in a dog crate. At the show itself the judge will want to check your dog over and see him in action moving around the show ring.

6 BREEDING ENGLISH SPRINGER SPANIELS

Breeding a litter of puppies can be very rewarding, but it can also be costly and time consuming. Each pregnancy will also put your bitch at risk, so you need to consider the pros and cons very carefully. You should not breed from your bitch if she has any health issues or faults that she would perpetuate in her puppies. You will want to make every effort to ensure that the puppies that you breed have sound temperaments, are healthy, and are good examples of the breed. You will also want to make absolutely sure that your puppies go to good homes.

Before you go ahead and breed your litter, you would be well advised to ask yourself some serious questions. Do you have the time to look after your litter until they go to their new homes (around eight weeks)? Are you knowledgeable enough to advise your puppies new owners about the various aspects of caring for their

ABOVE: *Will you be able to place your puppies in good homes?*

puppies, including their diet, training and health problems? Can you afford the veterinary bills for your bitch's ante-natal care and for her litter? Do you know enough to help the bitch during her labour? Could you afford for your bitch to have a caesarean if she needs one? Are you equipped to raise the puppies with everything they need including worming, vaccinations and socialisation? Most importantly of all perhaps, will you be able to place your pups into good homes and would you have the resources to take puppies back if the homes you sold them to prove unsuitable?

Many people breed from their Springer bitch because they would like to keep a puppy for themselves and most bitches sail through whelping and very much enjoy having puppies. You should not breed from your Springer

until at least the third time she comes in season, at approximately eighteen months old and ideally before she is three years old.

THE STUD DOG

The demands on dog breeders grow increasingly complex to ensure that future generations of dogs are bred responsibly. The over-riding consideration is the health of any potential puppies. This is particularly important when you are looking for a stud dog. He must have a good temperament, good health and be a good example of the Springer Spaniel. If your bitch came from a reputable breeder, go back to them and ask their advice about what stud dog to use. It is always best to use a proven, experienced stud dog. Predicting breed type and characteristics requires

69

experience. If you are new to dog breeding then you should seriously consider joining an appropriate breed club where you will be able to meet and talk to some very experienced breeders.

You should certainly take the time to go and see the dog that may become the father of your puppies. You should also show your bitch's pedigree to the owner of the stud dog so that they can approve of her. Ask what the stud fee is and what conditions will be included; for example, do you get at least two matings if necessary and if your bitch fails to have puppies, does the stud fee cover a free return? Most stud dog owners offer this. You then need to work out when your bitch will be in season and when the puppies will be born.

There is a lot of time and work with puppies, so make sure you are going to be able to give it when they are born.

MATING

New breeders need to concentrate on finding out when their bitch comes into season. If you don't realise until your bitch has been in season for several days, it may be too late. This is disappointing if all the plans have been made. You will need to check your bitch virtually every day for the start of her season. The first sign is the vulva swelling. Some bitches' vulvas swell and do not show any signs of red discharge, others will show very little red discharge. Count from the day her vulva becomes swollen, just in case she is a bitch that has clear seasons.

Once your bitch is showing colour wait until the discharge becomes paler until you take her to be mated. You can check this by using either a white tissue to dab the vulva morning and night to determine the colour change, or you can put a white cover on her bedding so that you can monitor the colour change. If your bitch does not show any colour change you will need to count the days after she comes into season; ten to twelve days after coming in season is probably the best guide. However, some bitches are ready to mate after just six days into their season and have produced puppies from this mating, but this does not happen very often.

Once the bitch has been mated, you must keep her away from other male dogs until she is completely out

ABOVE: *It is important that the mother eats well during and after the pregnancy.*

of season. It would probably wise to keep her away from any male dog all the time she is in season.

First-time breeders can also be nervous. Not everyone is aware that mating dogs "tie" or "lock" together during mating, on average usually for about twenty to thirty minutes. Sometimes dogs are locked together for hours, although this is very rare. It is usual to have your bitch mated twice, approximately forty-eight hours apart; once this is done take your bitch home and keep her secure and quiet.

Occasionally a bitch will, after being mated, have a red discharge from her vulva, even as late as three to four weeks after mating. This usually indicates that the bitch is in whelp and there is activity within the womb. In the early days of pregnancy nothing should be changed, so treat her normally.

PREGNANCY

A bitch is usually pregnant for sixty-three days or nine weeks, but you should be prepared for her to give birth up to five days early or four days late. You may be able to see that your bitch is pregnant from about three weeks, although some bitches do not show until seven weeks. Early signs of pregnancy are when her teats become pink or purple. She may also lose her appetite, and she may be sick. She may also become very quiet. On the other hand, she may show no signs at all but still could be pregnant. If you can see signs of her pregnancy very early, this may indicate that she is having a large litter. You should usually know whether she is in whelp or not by around six weeks.

As soon as you know that your bitch is pregnant, you need to change her diet from approximately five weeks onwards. As the puppies grow bigger, she will not be able to eat as much as she needs in just one feed. It is advisable to split her food into at least two meals a day, and up to four feeds a day towards the end of her pregnancy. It is very important to keep your bitch well nourished so that she will have the energy she needs to give birth. In the final two weeks, your bitch's exercise should be supervised so she is not overtired. Gentle exercise is good for her but car journeys should probably be avoided. Towards the end of the pregnancy your bitch will probably have a sticky clear discharge from her vulva; this is normal. Any other colour is not and may mean she could be aborting her puppies and needs to see the vet.

WHELPING

As your bitch's due date approaches, you should decide where she will give birth. This needs to be somewhere comfortable and quiet. It would be sensible to inform your veterinary practice that your bitch is due to whelp, then, if you do need to consult them in the middle of the night, they are better able to give you any help you need.

When your bitch goes into labour the best thing to do is to sit quietly near her and give her comfort and reassurance as and when she needs it. This stage of labour can last as long as twenty-four hours, and she may pant and tremble and dig up her bedding and look totally distressed. Don't worry, this is quite normal. You should only offer her clean water at this stage, as many bitches vomit during labour. Your bitch will then go into the next stage when strong contractions will start. She will start to push as they increase in intensity. Her first pushes will be light and get much stronger. Your bitch may also pass a water bag which will then break, producing a clear liquid. Soon after this the contractions will get stronger and a puppy should be born within 20-30 minutes. This second stage of labour can last between 3 and 24 hours with puppies being born within 20 minutes of each other, but there can be up to two hours between puppies. Mum will usually clean the puppy and bite through the umbilical cord. Some puppies are born tail first, but this isn't a problem.

If your bitch is busy delivering the next puppy, you should remove the membrane from the puppy and dry him with a clean facecloth. Rubbing will encourage him to take his first breath

ABOVE: *After giving birth help the new mother to go outside to relieve herself.*

and crying helps to clear his airways. You should also tie a piece of heavy thread around the cord approximately one inch from the pup's body, then tie another knot a little further from the first and use clean scissors to cut the cord between the knots. Be very careful not to cut too close to the puppy, and dip the end of the cord in tincture of iodine or chlorhexidine.

The third stage of labour is the passing of the placentas. You should count them to make sure that none are retained in the uterus. Some bitches eat the placentas which contain nutrients that help her body to recover.

If you are unsure how things are going, the bitch is straining, or a placenta is retained, you should call your vet immediately.

When your bitch's labour is finished, you should get the mother something to eat and drink, and help her to go outside and relieve herself. You should remove and replace the soiled nest covers and then give the new family some time alone. Your bitch will probably want to sleep while she suckles the puppies. This first milk is very important as it contains colostrum that contains the mother's antibodies and will protect them until they are old enough to be vaccinated. It may be wise for your vet to see the bitch and puppies soon after whelping. He will probably give the bitch an injection to ensure that any pieces of retained placenta are expelled. You should also get the puppies examined for any abnormalities.

AFTER THE WHELPING

If your bitch isn't interested in taking care of her puppies and doesn't show any concern for them for more than an hour you may need to take over looking after them. You should also consult your vet for advice. Hand-rearing may be necessary especially if the bitch doesn't seem able to produce any milk. Other bitches are fantastic mothers and don't even want to leave their puppies so that they can go to the toilet.

It is very important that your new mother eats well. After eating the rich afterbirths your bitch may refuse food for a while and may go off her food altogether. You need to tempt her with some tasty treats. It is often preferable to feed your bitch several small meals a day, consisting of really good quality food. She will also need to eat well to produce enough milk for her growing puppies.

ECLAMPSIA

Eclampsia is a life-threatening condition that results from the bitch's loss of calcium during pregnancy (making the puppy's bones) and in her milk. It usually happens within a few weeks of her giving birth. Small dogs with large litters have an especially high risk of the condition. It can be avoided by a good diet in pregnancy. Symptoms of this frightening illness (which can start very quickly) include panting, drooling, vomiting, restlessness, muscle spasms, convulsions, breathing difficulties, heart problems and seizures. Eclampsia is a serious medical emergency and your dog will need urgent treatment, which will usually include calcium. This can be given intravenously. Once treated, your bitch should make a full and speedy recovery. However, the puppies should be fed for at least 24 or 36 hours. If there is any recurrence, she should not suckle the puppies again.

ABOVE: *When puppies have accepted puppy milk move on to solids.*

ABOVE: *Your litter of puppies will need to be wormed.*

WEANING THE PUPPIES

You should start weaning the puppies between the age of two and three weeks. Worming is also one of the most important things at this time. Most puppies are born infected by worms which will prevent them from thriving. The puppies will need worming at two weeks of age. This can be done with a liquid puppy wormer that your vet will supply. They should be wormed twice more before the age of eight weeks. As you start to wean your puppies,

LEFT: *Most bitches sail through whelping and very much enjoy having puppies.*

you can give them saucers of warmed puppy milk several times a day. When the puppies have accepted the puppy milk you can move on to solids. This could be canned puppy meat or dried food formulated for puppies. This should be fed warm. Dried food should be soaked until the puppies' teeth are stronger when it can be fed dry. Your puppies should also have constant access to fresh water. This is particularly important if you are feeding dried food as this can make the puppies very thirsty. By the age of eight weeks your puppies should be fully weaned and eating and drinking independently. They will then be ready

7 HEALTH CARE FOR SPRINGERS

ABOVE: *The first step towards a healthy dog is to buy from a good breeder.*

When you take on a Springer, you should be very careful to buy a dog that comes from a healthy line of dogs that does not carry any of the hereditary conditions that can affect Springer Spaniels. A reputable breeder will have bred out any hereditary diseases in their stock. You should also make sure that you have good access to excellent veterinary care for your beloved pet. It is also a good idea to keep a selection of first aid materials on hand in case of injury. You

should also have a rectal thermometer to check his temperature. A dog's normal temperature is 38.3 to 39.2 degrees Celsius (101 to 102.5 degrees Fahrenheit). If your dog's temperature is raised by more than two degrees you should take him to the vet immediately.

HEREDITARY SPRINGER DISEASES

Although Springers are mostly happy and healthy, the breed is prone to several hereditary diseases. Responsible breeders do not breed from dogs afflicted with these conditions, so there is every chance that your puppy will not be a carrier for any of them. Forewarned is forearmed.

HIP DYSPLASIA

Is a serious condition that affects several breeds of dog, including Springers. This degenerative condition affects the hip joint of the hind legs and can be crippling. A puppy can be born with seemingly normal hips, but the symptoms of the condition can appear as he matures. The condition can cause pain and lameness. It can be diagnosed by an X-ray.

PRA BLINDNESS

Progressive Retinal Atrophy is a hereditary condition. The good news is that the potentially faulty carrier gene for this condition has now been identified. A simple DNA test, the Optigen test, can determine if a dog has the two faulty genes that mean that he will inevitably suffer PRA blindness. This is important information for breeders, as puppies born to two "clear" parents can never contract the disease. Affected dogs always become blind.

CENTRAL PROGRESSIVE RETINAL ATROPHY

This condition of the eyes can result in a loss of sight, although the peripheral vision is not lost.

RETINAL DYSPLASIA

This condition can result in retinal detachment. It is an inherited condition.

ENTROPION

Entropion is a painful condition in which a dog's eyelids roll inward, allowing the eyelashes to rub against the cornea and irritate it. The upper and/or lower eyelids can be involved, and the condition can occur in either one eye or both. A dog with entropion will squint and have an excessive amount of tears coming from the affected eye. While any dog can have entropion, there is often a genetic factor. When caused by genetics, the condition will show up before a dog's first birthday. Springers are predisposed to this condition, which can be surgically corrected.

FUCOSIDOSIS

Fucosidosis is a very serious disease of the nervous system that affects a few breeds including English Springer Spaniels. It is a hereditary illness that is characterised by deteriorating signs of the nervous system that progress over a period of several months, sometimes from an early age. Signs include loss of control of movement, a change in temperament, a loss of learned behaviour, a loss of balance, apparent deafness, visual impairment and depression. The disease affects young adults, usually between 18 months and 4 years of age. It is caused by the absence of an enzyme that is needed to break down complex compounds into simple molecules that the body can use. Fucosidosis can affect all English Springer Spaniels, but there is a DNA test that has been available since 1997 which needs only to be done once in a dog's lifetime. Affected dogs should not be bred from.

PFK (PHOSPHOFRUCTOKINASE) DEFICIENCY

PFK is an enzyme that converts sugar into energy to maintain normal cell function. PFK deficiency is an inherited illness that causes abnormalities in red blood cells and muscle cells. A symptom of this disease is dark urine and, in severe cases, pale gums (anaemia) or jaundice coupled with fever and poor appetite. Clinical signs often develop after strenuous exercise, prolonged barking or extensive panting, all of which are conditions that accelerate the destruction of red blood cells in affected dogs. PFK deficiency can present as anything from mild to life-threatening episodic illness. The most important treatment is to manage the dog's activity and stress levels. Where anaemia becomes critical, veterinary care is required to manage the condition until it normalises.

CANINE AUTOIMMUNE MEDIATED DISEASE

Dog's with an autoimmune disease have a faulty immune system that rejects normal body tissue and red blood cells. Unfortunately, Springer Spaniels have a genetic predisposition to the condition, which can cause anaemia and jaundice. Common symptoms include listlessness, depression, lethargy or collapse. To confirm the diagnosis a Coombs blood test is usually carried out to look for red cell-bound antibodies. The disease is treated with high doses of immunosuppressive drugs to lower the dog's immune response.

Summary

English Springer Spaniels are the oldest recognized breed of hunting dogs in the world. The breed has now separated into two distinct strains of Show and Working dogs. Both strains of Springer have their adherents and, given the right conditions, both can make wonderful family pets. From the excitement of collecting your puppy, to looking after the needs of your adult and veteran, this book will show you how to give the best possible care to your beloved Springer Spaniel.